AMS PRESS
NEW YORK

Reprinted from the edition of 1886, Cambridge
First AMS EDITION published 1971
Manufactured in the United States of America

International Standard Book Number: 0-404-04544-8

Library of Congress Number: 70-138943

AMS PRESS INC.
NEW YORK, N.Y. 10003

THE INFLUENCE OF ITALIAN

UPON

ENGLISH LITERATURE

DURING THE SIXTEENTH AND SEVENTEENTH
CENTURIES.

BY

J. ROSS MURRAY, B.A.

SCHOLAR OF ST JOHN'S COLLEGE.

BEING THE ESSAY WHICH OBTAINED THE LE BAS PRIZE, 1885.

CAMBRIDGE:
DEIGHTON, BELL, AND CO.
LONDON: GEORGE BELL AND SONS.
1886

PREFACE.

In the following pages an attempt is made to estimate accurately the nature and extent of the influence
exercised by Italy upon the English writers of the
Elizabethan and Stuart periods. General remarks upon
the Renaissance and its developments in different parts
of Europe have been avoided, except where they served
to illustrate the special subject of consideration. So
much has been written upon the Renaissance that it
seemed unnecessary to repeat what has already received
all but universal recognition. But it is possible to show
almost exactly how much English Literature owes to
Italy, as distinct from the debt due to other countries,
and from the undefinable influences which are abroad in
an age like that of the Renaissance. To show when
and how this debt commenced, how it accumulated, and
what the consequences were to the debtor is the object
of this essay.

CONTENTS.

THE FOLLOWING WORKS, AMONGST OTHERS, HAVE BEEN USED;

Sismondi, *Literature of the South of Europe.*
J. A. Symonds, *Renaissance in Italy.*
Collier's *Dramatic Literature.*
Ward's *History of English Drama.*
Symonds, *Predecessors of Shakspere.*
Warton's *History of English Poetry.*
Gosse, *Seventeenth Century Studies.*
Morley, *Manual of English Literature*
Symonds, *Italian Byways.*

I. HOMELY RIMERS.

'VERNACULAR literature all but dead[1],'—'Poetry and
Religion no longer capable of suggesting a genuine
sentiment[2],'—'style, metre, rhyme, language, art of every
kind is at an end'—such is the verdict usually pro-
nounced upon the English writers who flourished, or
rather did not 'flourish,' during the first quarter of the
sixteenth century. Some, however, hesitate to acquiesce
in the justice of this sentence. They discover germs of
life, nay, they discover signs of a healthy and vigorous
life where others see nothing but the symptoms of
disease, infirmity or death. In their opinion the poetry
of the period 'may be fairly described as the dawn
of a new day[3],' and they are inclined to associate it
rather with the glorious developments that took place
during the reigns of Henry VIII.'s children than with
the darkness and barrenness of the fifteenth century.

But however much critics may differ, they appear to
agree in one respect, namely, in treating this period as
one that is undeserving of any very serious or prolonged
attention. The text-books which claim to give to the
'beginner' a general survey of the field of English

[1] J. R. Green, *Short History*, p. 390.
[2] Taine, *Eng. Literature*, Bk. I. chap. III.
[3] Craik, *Manual Eng. Lit.* p. 191.

Literature may perhaps be excused for hurrying over
this portion with a passing observation or two, but it
may well be asked what reason there is for the neglect
from which it suffers at the hands of those whose
business and whose delight consist in drawing forth and
exhibiting those treasures which are to be found even in
the midst of the rubbish-heaps of past ages. Why has
the indefatigable Prof. Arber not given us, amongst his
numerous reprints, more of the verses written by the
contemporaries of Roy and Tyndal, 'doggrel' though
they be? Why has no Dr. Grosart yet appeared to
present the lovers of our old literature with sumptuous
editions of the complete works of Barclay and Skelton?

The reason is not far to seek, and perhaps from
certain points of view it is a fair one. The fact is that
the early part of the sixteenth century lies under a
double disadvantage,—first that of being undeniably
feeble in imagination and all that constitutes poetic
genius, secondly that of being in such close proximity
to the extraordinary outburst of literary activity which
found its precursors in Wyatt and Surrey, and rose to
its height in Spenser and Shakspere. The glimmering
of the pre-Renaissance night became darkness when
compared with the brilliancy of the galaxy which accompanied the shining of that 'bright occidental star'
which arose in the second half of the century.

But surely this fact, to anyone who wishes to have a
comprehensive view of literature, and of the causes
which make or mar its prosperity, will be an inducement
leading him to seek the motive-power and reason of so
great and so sudden a change, and in order to arrive at
this he is bound to examine the writings of the pre-
Renaissance authors,—to notice what are the characteristic differences between these and their Elizabethan

successors; to consider what influences the writers were subject to in each case, and which of these influences came from abroad, which from home, and whether the former or the latter exerted more power.

Our task at present is to make only one part of this investigation. We have to consider whether any influence from Italy was at work in England when Hawes, Barclay, Skelton, Heywood and their contemporaries represented English literature, and what effect, if any, such influence had upon their work.

Now if we were to select one feature of these writings as more prominent than any of the others it would probably be their plain, homely character—a plainness and homeliness peculiarly English, apparent alike in their matter, form and spirit. The topics with which they deal are mostly national and popular, or such as occasion frequent notices of the manners and life of the people, so much so that they have a considerable value for the historical student. Robin Hood is a favourite subject of reference. Cardinal Wolsey is a butt for satirical allusion. Chaucer and Lydgate, the poets of the people, are the models after which they are formed, and to which they pay tribute. Stephen Hawes knew much of their poetry by heart. Even when the themes are taken from foreign sources, only such are chosen as admit of being easily adapted to English taste; thus— the *Narrenschiff* of Brandt, translated by Barclay, was just the thing for the people who were catered for by William Roy and John Bale.

The homeliness of these authors is however far more noticeable in the style, metre, and diction which they adopt, and which is of an essentially popular rather than of a scholarly or courtly kind. The Chaucerian stanza is the favourite of Hawes and Barclay, who had neither

inclination nor ability enough to attempt other measures.
As for John Skelton—that 'rude railing rhymer'—
whatever may be thought of the merits of his verse it
cannot be denied that it has a vigour and plainness
which is peculiarly Saxon.   Let him defend himself :

> " For though my rime be ragged,
> Tattered and jagged,
> Rudely rain-beaten,
> Rusty and mooth-eaten,
> If ye take wel therewith
> It hath in it some pith."

But most of all in the tone and temper of what they have
written does the sturdy independence of English character, as yet unaffected by foreign influences of any
objectionable kind, show itself,—the character which
appears stamped on every page of honest Latimer's
sermons.   Through all their works there runs a tone of
seriousness, and in the poetry it prevails as much as
anywhere.   The *Pastime of Pleasure* is a long sermon in
verse.   'Pregnant' Barclay not only chose a didactic
poem for translation into English, but moralized therein
on his own account as well as on Brandt's.   Some of
Skelton's best pieces are his invectives against the
degenerate clergy, and his satires on the social and
religious abuses of the times.

Other characteristics of this poetry go to prove that
it was almost entirely the production of native forms
and ideas, and was very slightly affected by influences
from outside.   It shows a painful dearth of originality
of thought, a want of imagination, an absence of the
creative faculty.   Barclay is little more than a versifier
of other men's ideas.   Hawes merely follows in the
track of Chaucer.   Skelton, who is by far the most
powerful of the three, never soars into the regions of

fancy. Heywood is dull and obscure in his allegories[1], occasionally witty in his epigrams, and coarsely jovial in his interludes. There is no elegance of style, no grace of expression, no refinement of thought in these poets. Hawes was the only one who had any appreciation of the uses of Romance and Allegory, and what he had was borrowed from Dan Chaucer and 'Moral' Gower.

These facts are worth noticing because it is almost certain that during this time the foreign influences which were destined to produce such a remarkable change, or at least to aid in producing it, were already entering the country. The proofs of this are not numerous but they are sufficiently conclusive. It was at the Universities that the first signs appeared. In the reign of Henry VII. Italian poets were in demand at the Court, and Italian rhetoricians at the University. Cambridge was so 'destitute of skill in Latinity' that it had to procure the services of a certain Caius Auberinus, an Italian, 'for composing the public orations and epistles.' In the year 1488 we find one Cornelio Vitelli at Oxford, an Italian who had come 'to give that barbarous University some notions[2].' Three years later Grocyn, fresh from the teaching of the famous Politian, came to Exeter College. Colet and Linacre were only two out of a number of Englishmen who had visited Italy, and associated with the best known litterati of Florence and Padua. Travel to foreign Universities had

[1] Harrison (*Description of England*) very fairly observes with regard to Heywood's tedious poem called the *The Spider and the Fly* that "he dealeth so profoundly, and beyond all measure of skill, that neither he himself that made it, neither any one that readeth it, can reach unto the meaning thereof."

[2] Anthony à Wood.

become so common that Barclay thought it necessary to
enter a protest against the custom, not having any high
opinion of its results.   The nobility and higher clergy
seem to have made a practice of securing learnéd
Italians as tutors for their children, or even for themselves, and when John Fisher was recommended to send
for an Italian to teach him Greek, Erasmus dissuaded
him on the ground that these foreigners, however successful in imparting learning, did not promote good
manners.   At Court too, Italian manners, whether good
or bad, were being gradually introduced.   In 1512 'on
the day of the Epiphany, at night, the king with eleven
others was disguised after the manner of Italy, called a
Mask, a thing not seen before in England[1].'   Educated
men began to be dissatisfied with what they considered
the rudeness and barbarism of the vernacular, and sought
to enrich it with foreign words.

It is important to observe therefore that, notwith-
standing these innovating tendencies, scarcely any effect
was produced upon the generation of literary men
represented by Hawes, Barclay and Skelton, as far as
the form and substance and spirit of their poetry was
concerned.   Of course they were not unaffected by the
great movement that was then passing from Italy over
the whole of Western Europe—the 'New Learning.'
Skelton himself was no mean scholar and was honoured
by Erasmus with the proud title 'Unum Britannicarum
litterarum decus et lumen.'   But this involved no 'apish
imitation' of Italian ideas as set forth by Pulci or
Boiardo or others of the moderns.   If they imitated
Southern poets it was to Petrarch or Mantuan that they
went.   Skelton[2], in a list of poets of all nations whom

---

[1] Edward Hall, *Chronicle.*
[2] Skelton, *Garland of Laurel.*

he supposes to be gathered together in the presence
of Pallas, mentions among others "Boccaccio with his
volumys grete...Poggius Florentinus, with many a mad
tale...Plutarch and Petrarch, two famous clerkis," but
does not mention any of the Italians who had already
enriched their vernacular with many a lively poem, and
were even venturing to rival Petrarch in the writing of
sonnets. Barclay avows his obligation to Mantuan, but
shows no acquaintance with the recent developments of
Italian poetry. It is true that a few translations from
Italian authors were made during this period, but they
were made, in almost every case from the Latin, showing
that at present the influence was chiefly academical.
Thus Barclay's first three Eclogues were derived from
the *Miseriae Curialium* of Aeneas Sylvius, and the
large debts which Sir Thos. Elyot in his *Governour*
owed to the Italians were all due to the Latin works of
Pontano, Beroaldo and Patrizzi[1]. The fact that in 1532
there was printed a versification of Boccaccio's story of
Sigismunda and Guiscardo does not necessarily point
to any new Italian influence, for the story had become,
in a sense, English property, having been previously
translated as early as the fourteenth century, when, as
any reader of Chaucer knows, Boccaccio was well known
in England. Stephen Hawes is said by Warton[2] to
have 'become a complete master of the French and
Italian poetry,' but whereas the marks of his French
accomplishments are conspicuous in *Grande Amour*, it
is hard to find in his poems any trace of familiarity with
Italian. A few Italian phrases occur in Skelton, but
they prove nothing, for the poem in which they are

[1] See the very thorough edition of Elyot's *Governour* by H. Croft,
Introd.

[2] *Hist. Eng. Poetry*, III. p. 170.

found[1] was intended to be a 'mingle-mangle' of all kinds of words and phrases jumbled together. It has been supposed that to Skelton may be attributed the introduction to England of that species of poetry which was invented in Italy and received the title 'Macaronic,' but even supposing that the mixture of words from Latin with the vernacular is rightly described as Macaronic, it seems impossible that Skelton could have derived it from its inventor, for Folengo's *Macaronices* was not published till 1521 and Skelton died in 1529, so that even if the *Speake Parrot* was one of his latest poems, there is scarcely time for Folengo's idea to reach England.

If indeed it be a fact that Sir Thomas More derived the idea of his *Utopia* from Amerigo Vespucci's account of his voyages, then it must be confessed that this period owes at least one considerable debt to Italy, but this is no indication whatever that Italian books were being circulated in England, even had we forgotten the fact that the first book of *Utopia* was both written and printed on the Continent, and that Antwerp and Louvain were familiar with the Italians while these were still strangers to home-keeping Britons.

Our conclusion therefore must be that during the first quarter of the sixteenth century no perceptible change or development had taken place in English literature through the incoming of Italian influence. Perhaps we may assign 1529, the year of Skelton's death, as the epoch when the signs of a 'new departure' first appeared, in the altogether different poetry which will now have to be described.

---

[1] *Speake Parrot.*

II. COURTLY MAKERS.

The first distinct impetus in the direction of imitating
the modern Italian poetry came from the Court. We
have already seen how the germs of this movement
existed, how Italian poets were hired occasionally for
the amusement of the lords and ladies of Henry VII.'s
Court, and how Italian masks became fashionable early
in the reign of Henry VIII.   The latter king, in addition
to his fondness for pomp and gaiety, had an affection for
learning and the Belles Lettres, and his court soon
imbibed a taste for that refinement which was only to be
found in France and Italy, and the special home and
nursery of which was the land where Lorenzo de Medici
patronized Learning, Poetry, Sculpture and Painting,
and where Ariosto and Boiardo, Trissino and Sanazzaro
were already household names.   Men who had learnt to
admire the finished elegance and musical versification of
such poets were not likely to retain much love for the
ragged rimes of Skelton.   They began to try whether
their own language was not capable of becoming the
vehicle of sonnets, madrigals and canzoni like those in
which the ready Florentine sang graceful praises to his
mistress.   The two men who set the example of this
'Italianizing' were both courtiers, and the passage in
which Puttenham mentions their work, although well

known, cannot be omitted here, because it describes so exactly the general nature of the result which they achieved. He says[1] 'There sprang up a new Company of Courtly makers of whom Sir Thomas Wyatt the elder, and Henry Earl of Surrey were the two Chieftains; who having travelled into Italy, and there tasted the sweet and stately measures and style of the Italian poesy, as novices newly crept out of the schools of Dante, Ariosto and Petrarch, they greatly polished our rude and homely manner of vulgar poesy.'

The only correction necessary to make upon this passage is that no proof exists that Surrey was ever in Italy, this supposition having arisen merely from a legendary account that grew up around the name of the Tuscan Geraldine whose praises he sings. We know however that Wyatt did spend some time in Italy, and it is he whom we must regard as the first importer into our island of the lyrical love-poetry which has since formed so considerable a part of our literature. But the claims of Wyatt and Surrey in this direction are now so generally recognized that it will only be necessary to state, as a commentary on Puttenham's remarks, the exact amount that they contributed towards the development of our poetry, and the extent to which this contribution was supplied to them by Italy. Without attempting therefore to assign to each of these 'Courtly makers' his proper share in the result, and without trying to draw a comparison and a contrast between the two men—though this would be interesting enough—we may say briefly that the result they achieved was three-fold. First they brought the *sonnet* into use. Secondly, they introduced *blank-verse*. Thirdly, they proved that the language was capable of finer things than had ever

[1] *Art of English Poesie* in loc.

before been attempted, or, in the words of a modern critic, became 'the earliest exact writers of the modern tongue.'

But how much of this result was due to Italian influence? We may confidently answer—almost the whole of it. The fact is that these 'Chieftains' of the 'new company,' however talented, were under the complete control of their Italian masters. They are simply clever and graceful imitators, they produce nothing original. They can sing sweetly, but only the songs that their music-masters have taught them; they can compose elegantly, but only in the style that they learnt in their foreign schools. They have been so charmed with the ease and melody of Italian verse that they are almost exclusively occupied with attempting to reproduce it in their own tongue, and seldom think of daring to strike out on lines of their own. Thus Wyatt, when translating the sentiments of Alamanni, is not satisfied unless he faithfully copies also the style, and reproduces the *terza rima* of the original. In the same way Surrey, when the idea of translating Virgil into English verse occurs to him, not only chooses exactly the two books which Francesco Molza had recently turned into Italian, but imitates the *versi sciolti* of Molza in his blank verse. Again, why is it that both Wyatt and Surrey, in paraphrasing parts of the Bible, happen to choose the Psalms, and out of all the Psalms—those called the Penitential? Simply because they found that these Psalms had been versified by their models, Dante and Alamanni.

It may be observed too that almost all the sentiments of their smaller poems are echoes of ideas already put into verse by the Tuscan poets. Still it would be unjust to deny them the merits of freshness and vivacity, or to say that

LE BAS. 2

Wyatt did not think for himself; his pieces on 'How to use the Court and himself therein,' and on 'The mean and sure estate' contain reflections suggested more by his own life than by anything he had read in books.

One more comment must be made on Puttenham's statement quoted above, and that is to emphasize the force of his happy phrase 'Courtly makers.' It must not be supposed that the style of poetry introduced by Surrey and Wyatt speedily became popular. On the contrary, it remained for several years a fashion almost confined to the Court and its 'hangers-on.' Their poems were never printed till 1557, when they came out in *Tottel's Miscellany*, and until that time they were handed about in MSS. among the nobility and in the fashionable circles, beyond which the sensation produced by them rarely travelled. Thus amongst their imitators we notice the names of Lord Morley, Lord Vaux, Sir Francis Bryan, Viscount Rochfort, all of whom are supposed to have contributed to *Tottel's Miscellany*, or similar collections. But they seem to have had the effect of stimulating the study of Italian. We know that Elizabeth, Edward VI. and Lady Jane Grey were all well read in the language. Nor was this taste confined to the upper classes. From an inscription on a tomb dating 1537, it appears that a citizen's wife, Elizabeth Lucar by name, understood 'Latin, Spanish and Italian, writing, speaking and reading it with perfect utterance[1].' No doubt this good woman was a prodigy, but there are other things to show that during the last years of Henry VIII. an interest in Italian literature was growing. In 1545 Roger Ascham[2] complains of the introduction of outlandish words from the Italian into common speech.

---

[1] Strype's *Parker*, I. p. 358.
[2] *Toxophilus*.

About the same time a series of pamphlets appeared on the subject of Women and Wives, bearing various titles, which seem to have been suggested by the famous Italian story of *Belfegor* to which Macchiavelli had given such wide circulation. There were several Italians of culture resident in England, who would doubtless encourage at the Universities and elsewhere the study of their own unequalled literature. Peter Martyr, more properly called Vermigli, was at Oxford, and Bernardino Ochino was Prebendary of Canterbury.

But in spite of all this, the new movement failed to touch the people; it only stirred the few. It would require something more than 'Courtly makers' to popularize Italian authors or Italian fashions of writing and speaking among the sober, homely English folk with whom Heywood and Skelton were still favourites. Elegantly composed love-ditties, and sentimental sonnets were all very well for ladies and gentleman who had nothing else to do but sentimentalize, but they did not appeal to that desire for action, that eager thirst for incident and sensation which the awakening of a new life stirred in the minds of the people. How this feeling was appealed to we have now to see.

III. ITALIAN AND ENGLISH NOVELS.

Queen Elizabeth had scarcely completed her first measures for securing her throne and country from foreign interference, when the impetus was given, which resulted in a few years in the subjection of Literary England to the control of a foreign power. This impetus was given by the translation of Italian novels. In 1562 appeared rimed versions of some of Boccaccio's tales. In the same year was published Arthur Broke's verse paraphrase of Bandello's story of *Romeus and Julietta*. In 1565 came a translation of Ariosto's *Ariodanto and Ginevra*. In the next year appeared sixty novels from Boccaccio under the title *Paynter's Palace of Pleasure*, and this was followed in 1567 by a similar collection of 34 novels from Bandello and Cinthio. Between the years 1567 and 1587 the favourite tale of Boccaccio called *Filocopo* went through several editions. About 1576 came another collection of stories, entitled *A petite Palace of Pettie his pleasure*. This list might be continued much further[1]; but enough has been said to show

[1] e. g.

> 1576. Turberville's *Ten Tragicall Tales out of sundry Italians.*
> 1582. Whetstone's *Heptameron ;* containing Cinthio's tales.
> 1583. The first volume of Belleforrest's repository.
> 1587. The *Amorous Fiametta ;* licensed by the Bishop of London.
> 1597. *Two tales out of Ariosto,* etc.

that during the first part of Elizabeth's reign there was quite an inundation of Italian 'novels,' if they may be so called, though the 'novella' was very different from what we understand by a novel in these days. These tales were circulated throughout the country. They were published in cheap, portable forms, got up in an attractive style, with ingenious titles that were sure to arouse curiosity or interest. They found their way into the homes of almost all classes, and rivalled the new Geneva Bible and the Revised Prayer-Book in popularity. The man who was ignorant of Boccaccio was regarded more out of the fashion than he would now be who knows nothing of Victor Hugo or Sir W. Scott. Not even the *Arabian Nights* surpass the popularity which the *Ecatommithi* of Cinthio once enjoyed. So much interest in this kind of literature was aroused that many made up their minds to read it in the original, and the teachers of Italian found scores of eager and apt scholars. In 1567 a Dictionary 'for the better understanding of Boccaccio, Petrarch and Dante' had already gone through three editions, and between 1550 and 1600 four Italian Grammars were published. Every year numbers of copies of Bandello, Cinthio, the *Decameron* and similar books were brought over from Frankfort book-mart and found a ready sale at Stourbridge fair (the Cambridge students being eager purchasers probably), or at the St Paul's book-stalls.

The significance of this demand for the newly-imported tales is not difficult to understand when the character of the 'Novella' is known. That which chiefly gave it favour was its popular nature. As Mr Symonds[1] remarks : 'the Novella was in a special sense adapted to the public which during the age of the Despots grew up

[1] *Renaissance in Italy*, Vol. v. pp. 52, 53.

in Italy....Its qualities and its defects alike betray the ascendancy of the bourgeois element....Literature produced to please the bourgeois must be sensible and positive ; and its success will greatly depend upon the piquancy of its appeal to ordinary unidealized appetites.' What is true of the Italian citizens of the age of the Despots is, to a modified degree, true of the Londoners of the Elizabethan age. The shop-keeper and the apprentice, as well as the merchant, the banker, and the student found something that appealed to them in the tales of intrigue and adventure, of scandal and reprisal, of romance and mystery which had amused the leisure hours of the Florentine and the Paduan. This was the first time the people had had an opportunity of reading anything of the kind ; the *Decameron* indeed had been known in England before, but only through such versions as Chaucer's, and now the public was for the first time brought into direct contact with the sensationalism of Italian life.

There was however an influential minority who, so far from looking with favour upon this rapid spread of interest in Southern literature, protested against it on the ground that it tended to undermine the public morality. Indeed their fear was well grounded, as anyone who knows the outrageous sins against all decency and purity committed by the Novellieri will confess. Sometimes the Puritans, or those who in this matter at least sympathized with them, were successful in suppressing some of the more objectionable publications, as when in 1619 the Archbishop of Canterbury issued an inhibition against the *Decameron*. But at first the Censors of the press seem to have winked at the circulation of the most licentious tales, and it was left for Roger Ascham and one or two other honest guardians of the public morals to lift up their voices in condemnation. Ascham[1], writing in 1570, says that if he had his way he would burn them all: 'More evil is done by precepts of fond books, of late translated out of Italian into English, sold in every shop in London, commended by honest titles, the sooner to corrupt honest manners... There be more of these ungracious books set out in print these few months than have been seen in England many score years hence;...the *Morte d'Arthur*...was bad enough, but these ten times worse, being so subtle';... 'They think more of Petrarch and Boccaccio than of the Bible.' He regards the tales as a source of Atheism: 'One special point to be learnt in Italian books...to think nothing of God Himself'; and as tending to spread Roman Catholicism: 'More Papists be made by your merry books of Italy than by your earnest books of Louvain.' His language is not a bit too strong. There is no doubt that these 'Italian Prints' are responsible for very much that makes some of our Elizabethan literature unreadable in these days, and for much that must remain as a blot upon its brightness even when due allowance is made for the difference in the manners of those days. It may be worth while to call attention to the contrast between this period and the preceding in this respect. Skelton, however coarse he might be, was not impure, but many of the Elizabethans are wantonly gross, and the cause of the difference is mainly the contact with Italian corruption.

But on the other hand our literature owes to the introduction into England of these *Novelle* a triple debt of which Ascham was not aware, which, in fact, did not become manifest till after his death.

---

[1] *Scholemaster*, passim.

In the first place they gave the earliest stimulus to
novel writing. Previous to this time there had been no
attempt at prose fiction worth speaking of, More's
Utopia is an exception. The idea of writing fiction in
narrative does not seem to have occurred to Englishmen
until they had become familiar with the *Novelle*. But
then began imitations, and we may safely say that the
imitations were superior in some respects at least to the
originals. John Lyly, who wrote his famous *Euphues*
in 1579, is the man who bears the honour of being the
precursor of the race of English Novelists. Robert
Greene was one of the most prolific and popular of those
who followed him. Both had been 'Italianized' to a
higher degree than most of their contemporaries, and the
influence is apparent in almost all of their productions.
Greene's tales had immense popularity. Some of them
ran through several editions, and even held their ground
until the modern English novel had fairly come in to
supersede them. Gabriel Harvey, who was no lover of
Greene, grumbles at the favour they receive, and complains that they are driving out even the universally
admired masterpieces of Italy : 'Even Guicciardini's
silver history, and Ariosto's golden cantoes grow out of
request, and the Countess of Pembroke's *Arcadia* is not
greene enough for queasie stomachs, but they must have
Greene's *Arcadia*'...Nash bears similar testimony : 'glad
was that printer that might be so blest to pay him dear
for the very dregs of his wit.' These novelettes were
generally free from the worst blemishes of the Italian
models, and sometimes, as in the case of *Euphues*, were
written with a distinctly didactic purpose. Immense
as is the distance which separates a Greene from a
Thackeray we may therefore confess that as lovers of
'light literature' of the better class, we owe a debt of

gratitude to the former and his contemporaries for having pointed the way to the modern novel.

The second obligation which English literature owes to that Italian influence which accompanied the translation and imitation of the *Novelle* is the improvement of English prose writing,—the formation, in fact, of a new Prose.

Sir Henry Blount was using a pardonable exaggeration when he said that to Lyly 'our nation is indebted for a new English.' The first phase of the new style appeared in that peculiar kind of writing known as 'Euphuism,' the characteristics of which are not badly described by William Webbe as 'fit phrases, pithy sentences, gallant tropes, flowing speech, plain sense [1].' Anyone who compares this kind of writing, as exhibited in Lyly, Lodge or Sidney, with the prose of Elyot, Latimer or of Robinson's translation of the *Utopia*, recognizes the foreign element at once. Whatever was the chief influence which moulded the style of *Euphues* [2], it is certain that the richness, the affectation, the imagery, the elegant finish of the prose-writing which obtained currency in Elizabeth's reign were results of contact with Italy. But, like the poetry of Surrey and Wyatt, it was not a style that was ever likely to become really popular. It was chiefly a Court fashion. Side by side with its refined intricacy existed the simple straightforward prose of the people. Yet even this was to some extent affected by the tendency to cultivate a correct and elegant way of writing. *Hooker* was no euphuist, but his stately periods may owe something to the suggestions of the easy-flowing sentences of Lyly.

---

[1] *Discourse of English Poetrie.*

[2] Landmann, in his *Euphuismus*, considers that the style was partly due to the example of the Spanish *Guevara.*

Bacon is free from affectation, but he may have unconsciously learnt in the school of Euphuism how to write lucidly. Certainly the influence of this school survived in what has been called the 'Poetical Prose' of the earlier Stuarts; it is seen in the quaintness of Fuller, in the liveliness of Jeremy Taylor, in the magnificent sentences of Milton's *Areopagitica*, and in the 'splendid pedantries' of Sir Thomas Browne.

These two results, then, followed the introduction of the *Novelle* into our country—the creation of a prose fiction, and the commencement of a new prose style. But there was a third, far greater than these, and so important in its consequences, as well as permanent in its effect, that we shall be justified in referring its consideration to a special chapter.

IV. OUR DRAMATISTS' DEBTS.

It has been asserted above that Lyly and Greene may be regarded as the precursors of the modern novel-writers. But it is necessary to guard this statement against misapprehension. Not for a full century and a half did the actual beginnings of our novel-literature (as distinguished from romances) appear, and the whole interval between Robert Greene and Samuel Richardson was barren of any serious attempt to form a prose fiction of life, manners and character. Popular as *Pandosto* and *Menaphon* and *Perimedes* were, they did not produce any development of the species of writing of which they and *Euphues* were the best known representatives. What was the reason of this?

It was because another species of writing had almost simultaneously arisen, which in a few years completely outbid the novelette in the competition for popularity, and received such an enthusiastic welcome, that there was no chance of its rival being properly attended to. This was the Drama.

So much has been written upon the origin and growth of the English Drama that nothing need here be said, beyond what is necessary to illustrate the part which Italy played in this new development. One statement will be sufficient to show the extraordinary growth of its

literature, and it shall be that of Prynne, who in his
Histrio-Mastix (published in 1633) observes :—'Above
40,000 play-books printed within these last two years,
(as Stationers inform me) they being now more vendible
than the choicest sermons.' One remark may be offered,
amongst many that occur, as giving a reason for the
precedence which this form of composition took above
every other in the popular favour, namely, that it
satisfied, more than any other could do, that excitement,
that desire for Incident, Adventure and Action, that love
of sensationalism which so strongly characterized the
Elizabethan age.

Having prefaced so much, the question which we
have to answer is—what had the Italian *Novelle* to do
with the rise of the English Drama ?

Every reader of Shakspere, however uncritical, is
struck by the fact that the names of the Dramatis
Personae in so many of his plays are Italian, and that
the scene where the incidents occur is so often an
Italian town. Knowing little of the conditions of the
age in which Shakspere lived, and nothing of the history
of Italian literature, he wonders why this is so. He
turns perhaps to the Introduction of the Clarendon
Press copy which he happens to be reading, and dis-
covers that the poet is indebted for the leading incident
of the play to some Italian novel ; this rouses his
curiosity, he pursues his researches further, and even-
tually finds that this Prince of Dramatists, so far from
having invented out of his boundless imagination the
stories which have delighted the last three centuries,
was indebted not only for names and scenes, but for
many episodes and ideas, and sometimes for whole
plots, to obscure tale-books imported from Venice and
Florence. In his first surprise at this discovery his

opinion of Shakspere inclines to fall somewhat; he begins to wonder what would be left, if the borrowed elements were taken away; in that case, he thinks, we should have no *Othello*, no *Romeo and Juliet*, and probably no *Hamlet;* we should lose the *Merchant of Venice*, *Much Ado about Nothing*, and *Measure for Measure;* we should miss much that gives vivacity and interest to the *Tempest*, the *Taming of the Shrew*, and *Twelfth Night;* we should have to give up more or less of the *Two Gentlemen of Verona*, *All's well that ends well*, and the *Comedy of Errors*. All these plays, he finds, are derived either directly or indirectly, either in the whole plot, or in part of it, from translations of Italian novels. He cannot help imagining where Shakspere would have gone for his material, if these novels had never come into his hands. Would he have dramatised the Arthurian legends? Would he have been obliged to make the most of dry chronicles, homely ballads, and ale-house tales? Or would he have sought stuff for his genius to fashion into shape in the stories that were getting abroad about the wonderful lands of the far West? It may be idle to speculate in this way, but it is most important to recognize the immense obligation Shakspere owes to Italy. It is not necessary to make any apology for him; it was the best thing he could do perhaps. He could hardly help doing it. Italy fascinated him as it did many others. Here he found in rich abundance the very best material for tragedy and romantic comedy. Our opinion of his powers is not lessened. All poets borrow. Their greatness consists not in inventing the form, not in creating the skeleton, but in filling it with life.

What Shakspere did all the other dramatists of his times did also. In fact it was quite the orthodox

method of working up a play to start from a novel.
This custom commenced almost simultaneously with
the translation of the *Novelle*. Arthur Brooke in 1562
says that he had seen the argument of *Romeus and
Julietta* set forth on the stage ; but the earliest known
play derived from a *Novella* is the *Tancred and Gis-
munda* which appeared in 1568. A merely cursory
examination of the contemporaries and successors of
Shakspere will show how much they drew from the
same source. Thus,—nine of Beaumont and Fletcher's
dramas have their scenes laid in Italy, four of Massinger's, four of Ford's, and in all these the 'Personae'
are, of course, Italians. Ben Jonson in the first draft of
his *Every man in his Humour* gave Italian names to
the characters. Shakspere himself hints at the pre-
valence of the custom with perhaps a touch of satire[1]:
'His name's Gonzago : the story is extant and writ in
choice Italian.' Some of the most powerful of the
Elizabethan tragedies were based on these tales. Webster
worked up the horrors he found in Bandello, and produced his *Duchess of Amalfi*. Some of the novels
were especial favourites; thus the story of *Belfegor* as
told both by Macchiavelli and Straparola was the source
of no less than three plays—Dekker's *If it be not good,
the Divil is in it*, Ben Jonson's *The Devil is an Ass*,
and John Wilson's *Belfegor*. Even in the later Stuart
period this source was occasionally reverted to. In
Sir W. Davenant's *Platonic Lovers* the names are all
Italian, and his too is the *Just Italian*. In Farquhar's
The Twin Rivals, which came out in 1702, there is a
recommendation to a poet in search of a plot to 'read
the Italian' as well as the Spanish plays, and Dryden

---

[1] *Hamlet* III. ii.

in 1678 obtained some of the incidents for his indecent *Limberham* from a novel of Cinthio's.

If we now put the question 'what was the element of attraction that so strongly drew our dramatists to Italian sources?' we shall have no difficulty in determining the answer. Italy was at that time the home of the Heroic and the Tragic. It was, more than any other, the land of Adventure, Intrigue, Sensationalism, Scandal, Crime. The courts were centres of refinement, gallantry and subtlety; the Academies were nurseries of learning, but also of evil theories; the towns were full of turbulent life, and restless activity; the streets were constant scenes of strife and assassination. Mocking Atheism went side by side with devout Catholicism, cynical indifference watched the gorgeous processions of the pomp-loving Cardinals, while eager place-hunting and passionate Revenge dogged their footsteps with the dagger and bowl of poison ever at hand, and poets all the time went on singing dainty melodies of Love and Beauty. All this was known in England. The newest intrigue at the Vatican—the last scandal of the Court of Ferrara—the latest murder at Florence—the news on the Rialto—all this was eagerly looked for by those who made it their business to purvey exciting stimulants to the imagination of the public. For them no fiction could have charms equal to the wondrous facts of Southern life. None lent themselves more readily to stage adaptation. None could possibly be better subjects for Tragedy. Poets went over to Italy and came back full of poetic fervour and tragic sentiment. Those who did not go were almost equally affected by the contagion. In addition to the Tales they had the histories of Macchiavelli, of Guicciardini, and Contarini, in which they saw the life of Italy reflected. The very fact that most of the poets only knew Italy by hearsay helped to give a weird, romantic glamour to their conceptions. What went on in England was quite prosaic in comparison. True, there were events of romantic interest, such as those connected with the names of Mary Queen of Scots, and Amy Robsart, but no Elizabethan dramatist dared even allude to these. But in using Italian materials there was no fear, and the playwrights had free license to avail themselves of whatever would suit their purpose. The use which they made of their opportunity was not always such as will commend itself to the taste of the Nineteenth Century. They seemed to revel sometimes in depicting disgusting scenes, and in trying to rival, in sanguinary and revolting details, the horrors of such productions as Cinthio's *Orbecche*. But we must remember that they were only reproducing what actually went on in the land that fascinated them, and we may be thankful on the one hand that in England they could find nothing sufficiently horrible to inspire their awful Muse, and on the other that the really noble tragedians of this period, while retaining what was necessary for the completion of the plot and the full expression of the ideas, rejected *in most cases* those unnecessary accessories which were introduced to pamper the depraved taste which looked to Italy for the *Police News* of the day.

It follows from these considerations, and from the intercourse with Italy that has been already noticed, that the Drama would be likely to be influenced in other ways than merely by the *Novelle* supplying plots. There are several reasons for believing that other developments and characteristics of the Elizabethan and Stuart Drama were more or less of foreign importation.

We know that as early as 1565 Ariosto's Comedy

Gli Suppositi was translated. In 1578 a company of Italian Players was in England and performed before the Queen. Many traces exist in the Elizabethan writers proving their familiarity with Italian acting. Ben Jonson[1] mentions the 'extemporal plays,' which Whetstone[2] also remarks upon, observing that 'the Comedians of Ravenna are not tied to any written device.' Middleton, as is clear from his description of their acting in the *Spanish Gipsy*, had seen players of the same kind. Shakspere notices them, and Kyd[3] says,

> " The Italian tragedians are so sharp of wit
> That in one hour's meditation
> They would perform anything in action."

'Masks' had by this time become common, and were performed with great splendour, but they were still recognized as a distinctly foreign amusement :

> " Therefore I'll have Italian masks by night
> Sweet speeches, comedies and pleasing shows[4]."

Some of the more conservative onlookers did not altogether approve of this taste for outlandish novelties :

> " All eyes behold with eager deep desire
> These enterludes, these newe Italian sports
> And every gawde that glads the mind of men[5]."

But some of the most talented poets saw in these a new and inviting outlet for their efforts, and Jonson, Lyly, Chapman and Fletcher reproduced with considerable success the kind of pageant which had long amused the Milanese and Florentines at holiday-time.

Italian Comedy never seems to have been much known in England, but indirectly it had some effect. Massinger drew from it, and D'Israeli supposes that his

---

[1] *The Case is Altered.*   [2] *Heptameron.*   [3] *Spanish Tragedy.*
[4] Marlowe, *Edw. II.* I. i.   [5] Gascoigne, *Steele Glass.*

Empiric came from the same source as Molière's *Médecin*,
—namely the familiar *Dottore* of Southern Comedy,
another of the stock characters of which is imitated by
Gosson in his *Captain Mario*. We cannot forget too
that to Italy we owe nearly all the familiar figures of our
Pantomime,—the Zany, Harlequin, Pantaloon; Punch,
Mountebank, Scaramouch and Columbine are all Italians
by name and nature. The ballet came from Italy, so
did 'Puppet-plays,' and it was in Italy that women first
began to act on the stage.

There was one tendency visible during the reign of
Elizabeth, which, had it been stronger, might have
materially affected the character of our drama. This
was the influence of Classic example and Academic
rules. Some of the leading critics of that time thought
that the model of the Classic drama ought to be strictly
adhered to. Among these were Sir P. Sidney and
Whetstone, who, in his preface to the play *Promos and
Cassandra*, shows his preference for the Classical over
the Romantic method. In Comedy Plautus and Terence
were considered the best examples, and in England, as
in Italy, numerous imitations of their comedies were
produced,—a fashion which was perhaps encouraged by
the habit of producing plays at the Universities. The
same tendency to be guided by the examples of antiquity
showed itself in the attempts made by some purists to
naturalize the hexameter, and in the protests made by
men like Ascham, Puttenham and Milton against the use
of rime. Happily however for the development of a
true English literature, these attempts failed for the
most part. Though well-meant, they were contrary to
nature. It was putting new wine into old bottles to
clothe and hamper the bursting energy of English life
with antique methods and conventional measures. The

impetuosity and careless freedom of the early dramatists
refused to submit to the dictation of their elders. And
thus it was that there arose the grandest development
of all our literature of this period,—the Romantic Drama,
of which Marlowe is said to be the 'Father,' but of
which Shakspere is the life and soul. This is a peculiarly
English growth, and its origin is to be sought rather in
the general conditions of the time, than in any special
Italian or other influence. Italy had nothing to compare with the Romantic Comedy of Shakspere. It is
not indeed unlikely, as an eminent critic has remarked[1],
that the Elizabethan dramatists received, unconsciously
perhaps, ideas from the *Commedia dell' arte*, which
Shakspere formed into shape. This branch of Italian
literature, which at the outset was distinctly popular,
was in his time subject to the influence of the Academies.
But in England there were no such Academies, and the
dramatists had nothing to prevent them from seizing
and adapting for their own purposes whatever useful
elements they found in this *Commedia*. Chiefly it was
in the 'variety of effect which it was capable of producing
with a series of characters more or less fixed, so as to
preclude all deeper characterization[2]' that its value lay.
It has been already shown what an impression was
made in England by the improvisations of Italian
players. No wonder then if Shakspere, who probably
came up to London just at the time when this was
first observed, soon turned his attention to consider the
possibility of using the idea to produce something quite
different. A few years probably before he brought out
his first play, a well-known Florentine poet was attempting to strike out a new line in what he called *Farsa*, a
kind of dramatic composition which he thus describes :

[1] Ward, in *Hist. Dram. Lit.*, passim.   [2] *Ib.*

"The Farce is a third species, newly framed,
 Twixt Tragedy and Comedy. She profits
 By all the breadth and fulness of both forms,
 Shuns all their limitations[1]."

This 'sweet country lass,' as he was pleased to call
the new-comer whom he was trying to introduce to the
people, was therefore contemporaneous with the rise of
the Romantic Comedy in England.   The way had been
led by Lyly and Greene, whose fame rests as much upon
their dramas as upon their novelettes.   Lyly's plays
were quite a new departure, and are rightly called
'Court Comedies.'   Greene too, while imitating the
Italians, wrote plays that were distinctly original in cast,
and one authority gives it as his opinion that 'the
Romantic Play—the English Farsa—may be called in
a great measure his discovery.'   Lastly came that
wonderful 'warbler' of 'woodnotes wild,' who, finding
this 'sweetest prettiest country lass' waiting for a lover
and a champion, made her the 'bride-elect of Shakspere's
genius' and 'placed her side by side with Attic Tragedy
and Comedy upon the supreme throne of Art.'

A few words will suffice to trace the later influence
of Italy upon our Drama.   From 1630 to 1660 it is not
easy to find anything worth noticing, except, of course
an occasional borrowing of some Italian story.   There
was no fresh influence exerted, and simply for this
reason—that the age of the Seicentisti had commenced
in Italy, from which no good thing was to be expected.
But with the Restoration there began a new movement
in English dramatic circles.   Then it was that the
Opera first found a home in England.   In 1659 Evelyn
makes an entry in his diary to the effect that he 'went
to see the new Opera, after the Italian way, in recitative

[1] Quoted in Symonds, *Shakspere's Predecessors.*

music and sceanes.' Sir Will. Davenant was the enter-
prising dramatist to whom the introduction of this latest
Italian novelty was due.

" I would have introduced heroique story
In stilo recitativo"

says the musician in his *Playhouse to Let*. But the
opera proper was a long time in taking root here. As
early as 1594 it had made its first appearance in Italy
when Ottario Rinuccini brought out his *Dafne*, and it
was not really established in England till the beginning
of the eighteenth century. Even then it did not meet
with a very cordial reception. In 1706 John Dennis
says '(The operas) drive out poetry;...if an opera is to
infuse generous sentiment...it must be writ with force,
...but this is incompatible with music, especially in so
masculine a language as ours.' This however was not the
general opinion. John Dryden in his preface to *Albion
and Albanius* (1685) says: 'It is almost needless to
speak of that noble language in which this musical
drama was first invented and performed. All who are
conversant in the Italian cannot but observe that it is
the softest, the sweetest, the most harmonious, not only
of any modern tongue, but even beyond any of the
learned.' He goes on to confess his own debt to it:
' I may own some advantages which are not common to
every writer, such as are the knowledge of the Italian and
French languages, and the being conversant with some
of the best performances in this kind, which have
furnished me with such variety of measures.'

His allusion to the French language leads us to the
last remarks which it is necessary to make on the subject
of the drama. With the Restoration, French manners,
language and literature had entered England, and soon

became a part of cultured life as they had never done
before. Owing to the genius of the French stage at
this period, and the utter poverty of the Italian, it was
inevitable that the latter should give way, and forfeit the
supremacy which it had hitherto held. There was not
a single dramatist in Italy to compare with Racine,
Corneille or Molière. No wonder then that the Restoration Dramatists turned to France for inspiration. It
was partly in imitation of Corneille that Dryden made
rime the vehicle of tragedy, although he mentioned (as
instances of the same thing) the 'Spanish and Italian
tragedies, all writ in rime[1].' Otway, even when dealing
with an episode of Italian history in his *Venice Preserved*,
takes it from a French book, and in another play closely
imitates Racine. Finally the century was closed and
Italian influence practically ended with the rise of the
new Prose Comedy of Manners, under Wycherley and
Congreve, who derived their inspiration from Molière.

[1] Dedication to *the Rival Ladies*, 1663.

V. SIGNS OF THE TIMES.

As might be expected, the results of contact with the life of Italy were far more extensive than has yet been indicated. An immense impulse was given to the study of Italian literature of all kinds—history, philosophy, travels [1], as well as poetry and fiction. No one was considered accomplished in Elizabeth's Court unless he could quote Ariosto, or garnish his speech with Italian proverbs. No poetry was esteemed in literary circles unless it followed Italian precedents in sentiment and versification. Poets were fond of showing their acquaintance with the language of Romance by inserting Italian words in their verses. Those were considered the best courtiers who took most pains to carry out the teaching of Castiglione's 'Cortigiano'—their ' Hand-book of the Perfect Gentleman '; a treatise which had much to do with the forming of that school of elaborate politeness and gentility which Sir Walter

---

[1] In 1597 Abraham Hartwell translated a work on the Congo, written by Filippo Pigafetta in 1591.

In 1594 Wolf translated a book on the philosophy of Duelling.

Before 1611 a translation of Contarini's *Commonwealth of Venice* had been published.

Even Spanish and Arabian fiction first reached England through Italian channels ; e.g. in 1570 Sir T. North translated from the Italian version of the fable book *Calilah i Dummah*, and in 1612 Don Quixote was translated from the same language.

Raleigh and Sir Philip Sidney represented so well.
The prose-writers, as well as the versifiers, betrayed the
predominant influence; men like Nash and Gabriel
Harvey took pride in showing off their foreign accomplishments; thus in Nash we come across such words
as 'Bravamente,' 'Soldatescha bravura;' the more sober
Bishop Jewel speaks of the Pope as 'Cavezzo della
chiesa,' and Bacon alludes to him as 'Padre Commune.'
The terms 'Aretinism,' 'Macchiavellian,' 'Florentine,'
the titles clarissimo, magnifico, cavaliero, the phrases
'ragioni di stato,' 'chiaro oscuro' and 'mezzo tinto'
became common currency. So great was the demand
for a smattering of Italian, that John Florio was led
to publish hand-books which would enable would-be
Italianizers to pick up a little show of knowledge with
the least possible amount of trouble. These books
contained 'Frutes...of divers but delightsome tastes to
the tongues of Italians and Englishmen,'...'merrie pro-
verbes, wittie sentences, and golden sayings,'...'a perfect
Introduction to the Italian and English tongues.' As a
natural consequence of all this, the language became
enriched (or, according to some polluted) by the addition of many new terms to our vocabulary [1]. Several

[1] e.g.

balcony	carnival	farce (?)	manifesto	sonnet
baluster	carousal	fresco	motto	stanza
bandit	casemate	gallery	mountebank	stucco
bevy	casque	gazette	moustache	umbrella
bravo	cassock	gondola	opera	virtuoso
bust	cavalcade	grotto	palette	vista
canto	cavalier	harlequin (?)	pantaloon	volcano
caper	charlatan	lava	pedant	zany
caprice	ditto	macaroni	piazza	
capuchin	duel	madonna	scaramouch	
carbine	duet	madrigal	seraglio	

N.B. All these words occur in writers of the Elizabethan and Stuart

Italian words which are now thoroughly Anglicized entered the language during this period. A still larger number however of those which were then introduced failed to gain a permanent place, and are only to be found in works of the sixteenth and seventeenth centuries[1]. It was not without reason that Joseph Hall vented his satire on this tendency to overload the language with

> —" Terms Italianate,
> Big sounding sentences, and words of state."

Ascham and Wilson both complained of the 'strange words...which do make all things dark,' and lamented that 'some seek so far outlandish English that they forget altogether their mother's language.' But their remonstrances fell unheeded on the ears of men who were in love with everything Italian; 'Tut, saies our English Italians, the finest witts our climate sends foorth are but drie-brain'd dolts in comparison of other countries; whom, if you interrupt, they will tell you of Petrarch, Tasso, Celiano with an infinite number of others[2].'

The Universities seem to have shared the infection; Gabriel Harvey, describing the studies practised at Cambridge in 1580, says that the Italians are more read

periods. Others may be found in Skeat's *Etymological Dictionary*, pp. 752—757. Besides those derived directly from the Italian, there are several which were introduced from other languages through the Italian, e.g. caviare, candy, magazine, etc.

[1] e.g.

agraste	capriccio	galligaskins	punto
armigero	cullion	malgrado	retrait
ballat (=ballad)	duello	piastre	saffo
capreold			

and many more to be found in Spenser, Shakspere and the Elizabethan Dramatists.

[2] Robert Greene.

than Aristotle : 'You can't step into a scholar's study
but you shall find (these modern authors) on the table ;
…Macchiavelli a great man, Castilio of no small reputation, Petrarch and Boccaccio in every man's mouth,…
over many acquainted with Unico Aretino ; the French
and Italian when so highly regarded as scholars.'

The great Italian poets and critics (especially Bembo
and Politian among the latter) were on all sides looked
up to as the models of excellence, and as being on an
equal footing with those of antiquity.   Harvey judges
his friend Spenser's Eclogues by the standard of
Ariosto's works, and recommends him to take Macchiavelli, Aretino and Bibiena as his examples.   Sir P.
Sidney satirised the violation of the Unities of Time
and Place by the English dramatists, and considered
that the Italian models ought to be strictly copied.
The same critic objected to Spenser's 'framing of his
style to an old rustic language,' simply on the ground
that 'neither Theocritus in Greek, Vergil in Latin nor
Sanazzar in Italian did affect it.'   Sidney himself is one
of the best instances we could give of the control exercised by Italy over the cultured men of England.   In
his 'Arcadia' he imitated Sanazzaro not only in the
general ideas and structure of the work, but even in the
versification, attempting to copy the *sdrucciolo* rimes.
Even Spenser, who gave freer play to his own ideas, and
refused to be a slave to conventionalities, was at least in
his earlier years guided by the same masters.   'His
sonnets are Italian, his odes embody the Platonic philosophy of the Italians ; the stately structure of the Pro-
thalamium and Epithalamium is a rebuilding of the
Canzone, and his Eclogues repeat the manner of
Petrarch's minor Latin poems[1].'

[1] Symonds *in loc.*

VI. ENGLISH AND ITALIAN EPICS.

The name of Spenser suggests the next division of our investigation.

It would have been passing strange if, while sonnets, novels, pastorals and comedies from Italy were producing a fertile harvest of literature of the same kind in England, there had been nothing to correspond to the magnificent masterpieces of the Cinque Cento—the 'Orlando Furioso' and the 'Gerusalemme Liberata.' The former of these grand poems was first published in 1516 and soon attained a European reputation. Everywhere the name and fame of 'Tuscan Arioste' became familiar. His poem was printed in small handy volumes so that it might be the pocket companion of the traveller; it was customary to learn whole stanzas by heart; the gondoliers of Venice sung his verses as they plied their boats, and the apprentices of London vaguely associated him with all that was splendid and romantic. The complete poem was first translated into English by Sir John Harrington in 1591, in 'Heroick verse'; extracts indeed had been rendered as early as 1565, but there is nothing to prove that previous to 1591 any worthy attempt had been made to put Ariosto within the reach of the generality of English readers.

The 'poet of conduct and decorum,' Torquato Tasso, published his 'Gerusalemme' in 1581, and, as far as we know, the first translation, consisting only of 5 cantos, was by R. Carew in 1594, and the whole poem by Fairfax in 1600.

Thus a period of sixty-five years elapsed between the publication of Ariosto's great work, and that of Tasso's. It is a coincidence worth calling attention to that almost exactly the same length of time elapsed between the two Epic poems which occupy such conspicuous places in the English literature of the sixteenth and seventeenth centuries—the Fairy Queen of Edmund Spenser, and the Paradise Lost of John Milton. Is it pushing the analogy too far to fancy that there was a further correspondence, and that, as the poet of the Elizabethan age took the romantic Ariosto for his model, while admiring the recent genius of Tasso, so the poet of the Commonwealth took the lofty Tasso for an example, while acknowledging the power of the earlier Ariosto? However this may be, it is certain that Spenser and Milton must be considered together, as having been the two men among all the hundreds of miscellaneous writers and all the scores of talented 'makers' of their times, who were most effectually moved by the inspiration coming from the 'Orlando' and the 'Jerusalem.' All admired these writings, many imitated them, many stole from them ; a few produced really good copies of their ideas and pictures, but only these two succeeded in handing down to posterity, in poems which are prodigies of genius, the fragrancy of the southern influence which was about them when they wrote. In fact it almost seems as if the minor poets, conscious of their inferiority, purposely refrained from attempting to emulate the feats of those two giants of

the Italian Renaissance, and thus left the field clear
for the only men who were capable of equalling, if not
surpassing them. The 'smaller' men occupied themselves with the smaller kinds of poetry; they produced
innumerable performances of the lyric and pastoral kind,
but seldom aspired to the epic. Spenser and Milton
on the other hand were both above the 'smaller' poetry,
and were conscious of it. Though they gave way to the
fashion of their times, and wrote eclogues and sonnets,
they felt that this was not their vocation. Spenser was
dissatisfied with the 'small' writing that was so much
in vogue; he was no lover of euphuistic pedantry or
foreign affectation; he longed to produce something
that should be majestic in simplicity and earnest in
purpose. In the same way Milton's soul rose far above
the petty conceits, the far-fetched trivialities which
characterised the poetry of the early Stuarts,—the
poetry 'that flows at waste from the pen of some vulgar
amorist, or the trencher fury of a rhyming parasite,' and
sought satisfaction for his yearning genius in an epic
which should soar out of the domains of a conventional
Cupid, and rise to the heights of the

> "Immutable, Immortal, Infinite,
>   Eternal King."

It was but natural that, with such thoughts as these,
Spenser and Milton should be attracted by the two
poets who had lately arisen in Italy to cultivate the
stately muse of Virgil and Dante, and that they regarded
Ariosto and Tasso as models worthy of imitation. Let
us hear their own testimony. Spenser, writing to Sir
W. Raleigh to expound the object of his Fairy Queen,
says:

"I have followed all the antique poets historicall: first Homer, who in the persons of Agamemnon and Ulysses hath ensampled a good governour and a vertuous man,...then Virgil, whose like intention was to do in the person of Aeneas: after him Ariosto comprised them both in his Orlando: and lately Tasso discovered them again."

Here Spenser evidently regards the last named poets as on an equal footing with the great epic writers of anti-quity. From Gabriel Harvey we further learn that Spenser had set before him as his deliberate aim to 'overgo' the Orlando Furioso in his 'Elvish Queen.'

So much for Spenser's own acknowledgment of the debt he owed to Italy. But Milton is far more explicit and interesting in the account he has left us of the thoughts that Tasso inspired him with, and the following extracts from this account will be sufficient to show that however much meaning may be assigned to the state-ment, made to Dryden in his latter days, that in writing the *Paradise Lost* 'Spenser was his original,' the first suggestions to compose some such epic came partly, at least, from the Italians whom he loved so well. He says:

"In the private Academies of Italy...I began to assent...to an inward prompting...that I might perhaps leave something so written, to after times, that they should not willingly let it die....I applied myself to that resolution which *Ariosto* followed...to fix all the industry and art I could unite to the adorning of my native tongue." (He mused what to attempt—) "whether that epic form whereof the 2 poems of Homer and those other two of Virgil and *Tasso*, are a diffuse, and the book of Job a brief model....And lastly what king or knight...might be chosen in whom to lay the pattern of the Christian hero. And as *Tasso* gave to a prince of Italy his choice...etc.[1]"

It is surely significant that it was in Italy that he first distinctly conceived the idea of an epic as his life's work, and that it was to an Italian, his friend Giovanni Dio-dati, that he first communicated the idea.

When we proceed to examine the poems themselves,

[1] Milton, *Reason of Church Government.*

to see what witness they give as to the source of inspiration, we find abundant proof that the Italian epics were vividly present to the minds of the English poets.

We shall mention a few of the most striking of these proofs. To take Spenser first: although the general design of the *Fairy Queen* may be due, as has been suggested, to a French work[1]; yet its style shows unmistakeably a following of Ariosto, and the stanza in which it is written is probably a modification of that poet's 'ottava rima.' If he derives much from the Arthurian legends, he derives still more from the Tuscan's versification of the Charlemagne Romance. If the *Red Cross Knight* and *Una* are the author's own ideas, *Archimago* and *Duessa* are borrowed from Italy. The allegory indeed is, almost throughout, his own, but incidents, personages, illustrations are frequently taken from the rich stores of his foreign models. For instance that musical stanza in the last canto of Bk. II. in which is described the concert of all kinds of melodious sounds, where

—" consorted in one harmony,
Birds voices, instruments, winds, waters, all agree,"

is taken from Tasso, and at the very outset of the poem we discover an imitation of Ariosto, in the announcement that he is about to

—"sing of knights and ladies gentle deeds,"
and that

"Fierce wars and faithful loves shall moralize my song,"

passages which are suggested by

"Le donne, i cavalier, l'arme, gli amori,
Le cortesie, l'audaci imprese io canto[2]."

---

[1] *Le libre de droit d'armes*, pub. 1488.   [2] *Orlando Furioso*, I. i.

Sometimes he candidly acknowledges his debts, as when
he mentions

> —"that same water of Ardenne,
> The which Rinaldo drank in happy hour,
> Described by that famous Tuscan pen."

In Milton's case the resemblances are not so frequent
or obvious, but there is no mistake about their being
there.   His choice of blank verse was certainly a devia-
tion from the example of Tasso, yet in his Preface to
the *Paradise Lost* he gives as one apology for not using
what was then the common vehicle for poetry 'that not
without cause some both Italian and Spanish poets of
prime note have rejected rhyme both in longer and
shorter works.'   Nor can it be said that in the characterization of his Personae—as, for instance, Beelzebub,
Michael, Gabriel,—any certain marks of non-originality
can be pointed out.   These are peculiarly Milton's own
creations.   But in almost every book there are passages,
which, while stamped with the charm of Milton's inimi-
table descriptive power, betray at the same time the
incorporation of famous 'tit-bits' of Ariosto and Tasso ;
e.g. the beautiful description of Eve's bower :

> —" On either side
> Acanthus, and each odorous bushy shrub
> Fenced up the verdant wall; each beauteous flower,
> Iris all hues, roses and jessamin
> Reared high their flourish'd heads between, and wrought
> Mosaick; underfoot the violet,
> Crocus and hyacinth, with rich inlay
> Broider'd the ground, more colour'd than with stone
> Of costliest emblem[1]."

This is just in the style of the rich word-painting in
which Tasso loves to indulge.

Again, in the description of the single combat

[1] *P. L.* Bk. IV.   [2] *P. L.* Bk. VI.

between Satan and Michael, Milton proves, that however much he despised that idea of Epic poetry which
considered wars to be

> —"the only argument heroick,"

and admired most

> —"chief mastery to dissect
> With long and tedious havock fabled knights
> In battles feign'd[1],"

yet he was not insensible to the charm of that military
and chivalrous ideal of life with which even the sternness
of Puritanism had something in common.

Some few passages may be instanced as close imitations,—occasionally almost verbal translations from the
Italian, thus, the passage

> "What though the field be lost?
> All is not lost; th' unconquerable will,
> And study of revenge, immortal hate,
> And courage never to submit or yield "—etc.[2]

is from Tasso IV. 15.

The striking lines in which he describes the Limbo,
where are found

> "Both all things vain, and all who in vain things
> Built their fond hopes of glory or lasting fame," etc.[3]

may be compared, almost line for line, with Ariosto's
description of the Valley of Vain Things:

> "Le lacrime e i sospiri degli amanti,
> L' inutil tempo chi si perde a giuoco
> E l' ozio lungo d' uomini ignoranti,
> Vani disegni che non han mai loco,
> I vani desideri sono tanti,
> Che la piu parte ingombran di quel loco;
> Ció che in somma quaggiù perdesti mai,
> Là su salendo ritrovar potrai[4]."

[1] *P. L.* Bk. IX.
[2] *P. L.* Bk. I.
[3] *P. L.* Bk. III.
[4] *Orl. Fur.* XXXIV. 75.

Nor was his account of the sympathy of the angels in man's woes[1] written in unmindfulness of Ariosto's

> "Come gli ascoltâr l' anime sante,
> Dipinte di pietade il viso pio,
> Tutte miraro il sempiterno Amante[2]."—

He borrows also from Ariosto the idea of the Devil inventing artillery, and compares the hosts of Satan to those who 'jousted in Aspramont.'

But it is possible that Milton owed more than all this to Italy. In 1617 a kind of Mystery Play in five acts entitled *Adamo* was produced by the Italian poet Andreini, in which Adam and Eve, the hatred shown by Lucifer and the Devils, the Fall, the characters of Hunger and Death, the sympathy with man of the unfallen Angels, and many other points similar to those occurring in the *Paradise Lost* appear. It is said that Rolli, when in London in the beginning of the eighteenth century, heard that Milton, after taking part in a representation of this play of *Adamo*, thought of making a tragedy of it. Voltaire makes an addition to this account, saying that Milton actually composed a part of the projected tragedy; he heard it from several Englishmen, who had themselves heard it from Milton's daughter. Whatever we may think of this story, (and we are at least sure that Milton's original idea was to treat the subject dramatically), it is likely enough that his knowledge of Andreini's play led him to decide upon the theme which he finally adopted for his epic. And if this is so we have here another instance of the way in which Italian authors supplied English poets with the materials for their very best performances.

Apart from the *Paradise Lost* there are various

---

[1] *P. L.* Bk. x.   [2] *Orl. Fur.* XIV. 74.

indications of Milton's attachment to Italy. In his treatise on Education he recommends that boys should learn Italian, which he considers might be 'easily' done 'at any odd hour.' To two of the sweetest lyrics that the English language owns he gave Italian titles. He wrote sonnets in Italian, and several of his shorter poems bear traces of the Italian manner.

It would be wrong to leave Spenser and Milton without stating, at least briefly, the immense distance which separated them from the Italian authors as regards their purpose in writing. The chief aim of Ariosto and Tasso was to amuse, and they were not very careful about any other end; the chief aim of Spenser and Milton was to instruct, and they always kept this end in mind. 'To fashion a gentleman or noble person in vertuous and gentle discipline,' says the Poet-exponent of the true 'Euphuism,' 'is the generall end of all the booke.'

Milton takes a still higher strain:

> —"What in me is dark
> Illumine; what is low raise and support,
> That to the highth of this great argument
> I may assert Eternal Providence,
> And justify the ways of God to man"—

Such is the invocation of the Prophet of the Commonwealth. How utterly different from the impudent hypocrisy of the 'Divino' Aretino, or the easy-going wantonness of an Ariosto or Trissino! The contrast between the ideals of the English and Italian authors is worth the attention of any one who wishes to appreciate the real worth of English Literature, and can only be overlooked by those who strangely consider that artistic beauty of style, perfection of form and prettiness of sentiment constitute the excellence of 'Divine Poesy.'

But what could be expected from the poets who were brought up in the atheistic and dissolute courts of Ferrara and Florence? Ariosto and Tasso, with all their richness and elegance, with all their beauty of idea and execution, are marred from first to last by wanton impurity of thought and wilful licentiousness of language. They have rarely a genuine thought for anything higher than the gratification of desire; their only real allegiance is offered to

—"That law of gold,
That glad and golden law, all free, all fitted,
Which Nature's own hand wrote—What pleases is permitted."

Spenser, on the other hand, makes it one of his chief objects to inculcate self-restraint and purity of heart and life; when he describes chastity as

"that fairest virtue, far above the rest[1]"

he does so honestly, and not merely for the sake of pay-ing the Virgin Queen a pretty compliment.

The same contrast is seen from another point of view when we contrast the levity and reckless gay-heartedness of the Southerns with the serious tone that characterizes Spenser and Milton, and which, with the former, took shape in the personification of the Christian virtues (an idea quite alien to Italian methods), and with the latter, in the whole conception of the *Paradise Lost.* 'Not a ripple of laughter,' says the historian of the English people, 'breaks the calm surface of Spenser's verse[2].' M. Taine, whose French vivacity cannot under-stand our island-gravity, would attribute this difference to the dull foggy atmosphere in which the heavy Briton is condemned to dwell, as contrasted with the sunny skies of the south, but apart from all reasoning of this

---

[1] *F. Q.* III. Prelude.   [2] J. R. Green, *Short History*, p. 417.

kind, it is very probable that Spenser's seriousness was partly, at least, caused by the outrageous lengths to which Italian recklessness and godlessness had gone, and by the not unreasonable fear that his beloved England might, under the contaminating influence of foreign libertinism, be brought to a like condition. On every side he saw the moral degradation of Poetry. His friend Sidney had seen it too, and sorrowed over it, as a true lover of poetry must, to see it dragged in the mud. 'The comedies rather teach than reprehend amorous conceits, the lyric is larded with passionate sonnets, the Elegiac weeps the want of his mistress.' Hall, whose satires were published about the same time as the second part of the *Fairy Queen*, speaks in far more slashing terms :

> "Did never yet no damned libertine,
> No elder heathen, nor new Florentine,
> Tho' they were famous for lewd liberty
> Venture upon so shameful villainy."

Even the best of Spenser's contemporaries were in danger of prostituting their genius in order to gratify the depraved taste of the age—a taste engendered chiefly by the 'wanton books' which good bishop Alley had condemned as early as 1559. 'What is so expedient unto a Commonwealth,' said the Bishop, 'as not to suffer witches to live? And—I pray you—be not they worse than a hundred witches that take men's senses from them[1]?' Since his time the evil had grown apace. It had become fashionable to write verses urging a life of pleasure at the expense of virtue, and the literary world was full of pieces after the style of the elegant lyric of Lorenzo de Medici, the burden of which is

---

[1] See Prynne, *Histrio-Mastix*.

> "Youths and Maids enjoy to day!
> Nought ye know about to morrow."

Shakspere, who, as the author of *Venus and Adonis*, cannot be altogether exonerated from blemish in this respect, exactly describes the nature of the evil and its source :

> —"Then there are found
> Lascivious metres, to whose venom sound
> The open ear of youth doth always listen;
> Report of fashions in proud Italy,
> Whose manners still our tardy apish nation
> Limps after in base imitation."

It was with a deep sense of this corruption of manners and degradation of poetry that Spenser wrote his *Fairy Queen*. He and Milton are the Poets of the Puritan movement in its best and most liberal phases. They would have been poets had they never known a word of Italian, and never tasted the 'sweet and stately measures' of the southern poetry; they would have been 'Puritans' had there never been any imported vices from Rome and Florence to rouse their indignation, but it is open to question whether they would ever have had such a hold upon the people's love and reverence had they not been enabled, by their appreciation of the Romantic epic of the south, to appeal to the sentiments and associations which were uppermost in the minds of their contemporaries, and which will continue to exercise a charm, so long as Strength and Beauty are admired, and Hero-worship endures.

One word about the two Prose epics of the seventeenth century. Is it possible that the Bedfordshire Tinker who gave to Puritan England a 'Christian' for an Orlando, and a 'Mansoul freed' for a Gerusalemme Liberata, had read Fairfax's translation of Tasso, or

Harrington's of Ariosto ?   Unlikely as this may appear
at first sight, there is something to be said for it.   At
any rate the author of the *Pilgrim's Progress* and the
Holy War must have been acquainted at first or second
hand with the *Fairy Queen*, and so indirectly he experi-
enced the influence of the Southern epics.   Thus, after a
lapse of 200 years the romance first propagated in a
profane burlesque by the mocking Pulci, having passed
through all kinds of treatment, was fashioned by a
homely local preacher into a text book of earnest
religion.

VII. ENGLISH AND ITALIAN LYRICS.

On the lighter poetry of the latter part of the sixteenth and the first half of the seventeenth century
a marked effect continued to be produced by the fashion
of imitating Italian writers. Hallam, in noticing the
'remarkable sweetness of modulation,' which characterizes some of the poetry of Elizabeth's last years, seems
to agree with the opinion that this is to be attributed to
'the general fondness for music.' A cause which is at
least as likely may be found in the general fondness for
the melody of Italian lyrics. Other less commendatory
characteristics showed themselves in the early Stuart
period. Cowley's youthful poems contained imitations
of the Italian conceits; the puritan Marvell was not free
from their influence, and the same taste appears as late
as Dryden. One of Crayshaw's largest pieces is a translation from Marini's *Strage degli Innocenti*[1] and some of
Herrick's liveliest lyrics, such as ' *To live merrily and to
trust to good verses*,' are free reproductions of sentiments peculiarly Italian,—sentiments of which his better
self repented when he wrote

> " My unbaptizéd rhymes,
> Writ in my wild unhallowed times."

It is interesting to observe how Marvell, while attracted
by the graceful form and fancy of Italian poetry, and
adopting much of its method, rejects and condemns its

---

[1] Gosse, *Seventeenth Century Studies*, p. 157.

ungracious licentiousness; how pure and noble is the
tone of his dialogue - poem *Clorinda and Damon,*
(where the echo device is brought in very cleverly,) or
the dialogue between the Soul and Pleasure, where all
seductive charms fail to entice the soul, for

> "Nature wants an art
> To conquer one resolved heart."

There were however two kinds of poetry in which
the example of Italy was particularly strong.

One of these was the style which prevailed in the
first two reigns of the seventeenth century, and was
adopted by Donne, Lovelace, Crayshaw, Herrick, Herbert and several others; a school of writers whom Dr
Johnson christened 'Metaphysical,' whom others call
'Fantastic,' and yet others prefer to describe as flourish-
ing in the 'Decline of Elizabethan poetry.' In one
sense at least the last phrase pretty accurately describes
the school, for the kind of writing which they practised
was a corruption of the Euphuism of Elizabeth's court.
For laboured similes, far-fetched conceits, and a tendency
to sacrifice clearness of thought to cleverness of expression the verses of John Donne were the lineal descend-
ants of Lyly's Prose.

But some of the adherents of this school of poets
followed another example. They derived much of their
manner straight from Italy, where Marini, at the beginning of this century, was creating quite a sensation by
setting a new fashion of verse, its chief features being
whimsical comparisons, abundance of antithesis, and
concetti, and pompous descriptions. Crayshaw was a
Marinist, and probably Herbert, Carew and Herrick
were not unacquainted with the poems of this new leader
of fashion.

As being akin to this kind of writing may be mentioned the 'Emblems' of Quarles and similar writers. The liking for this kind of composition seems to have been first called forth by the Latin verse Emblems of Andrea Alciati, published about the middle of the sixteenth century; these were soon translated into Italian and French, and produced numerous imitations, e.g. those of Juan de Horozco in 1591. But their religious tendency made them special favourites in England, where Quarles and Wither found a large circulation for their little books.

Anagrams came into fashion in Queen Elizabeth's time; Puttenham tried to make one on her name, remarking that 'this conceit is well allowed of in France and Italy.' The idea too, of writing verses in various shapes first came to Puttenham when he was in Italy, as quite a novelty.

The second species of Poetry in which Italian influence was conspicuous was the Pastoral. Ever since the appearance in 1502 at the Neapolitan Court of Jacopo Sanazzaro's *Arcadia* this kind of writing had been enjoying a popularity which rather grew than diminished as the years went by. By Sanazzaro 'a literary Eldorado had been discovered, which was destined to attract explorers through the next three centuries[1].' In England one of the first explorers was Sir P. Sidney, who devoted himself to giving to his countrymen a poetic Romance exactly in the style of Sanazzaro. Lyly in his *Gallathea*, Greene in his *Morando*, Lodge in his *Rosalynde* made use of the new mine that had been opened, and Spenser spent his youthful energies upon *The Shepherd's Kalendar*. A fresh impetus was given by the appearance of two other Italian models—Tasso's *Aminta* in 1581, and Guarini's

[1] Symonds, *Renaissance in Italy*, Vol. v. p. 197.

Pastor Fido in 1585.   The popularity in England of the
latter is testified to by Ben Jonson (who himself could
write gracefully in the Pastoral method):

> "Here's Pastor Fido,...
> All our English writers,
> I mean such as are happy in the Italian,
> Will deign to steal out of this author, mainly[1]."

It is rather curious therefore that no translation of
this work appeared until Sir Richard Fanshawe brought
out his version in 1647.   The imitations, however, were
almost countless.   Every poet tried his hand at the
style.   Some of these productions were very poor affairs,
but others were fully deserving of the encomiums they
received; most of all, the *Faithful Shepherdess* of Fletcher.
Milton in *Comus*, Marvell in *Thyrsis and Dorinda*,
Wither in the *Shepherd's Hunting*, wrote with a grace
and prettiness which had never been equalled before in
the English language.   In the hands of Wither and
Browne especially, the Pastoral met with a sympathetic
treatment which saved it from becoming entirely conventional; they were inspired with a genuine love for
the natural beauty of the Country, and there is a simple
freshness in Browne's *Britannia's Pastorals* which we
miss in the courtly performances of the Italian writers.
Wither deserves notice for the bold stand which he made
against the conservative and imitative tendencies of the
day:

> "Pedants shall not tie my strains
> To our antique poets' veins;
> *   *   *   *   *
> Being born as free as these,
> I shall sing as I shall please."

A protest like this was seasonable and useful.   There

---

[1] *Volpone*, III. 2.

was a danger in Wither's time of an Academy, or something of that kind, being established, which should dictate to every one what was good poetry and what was not, and which should prescribe regulations for all kinds of composition. Such a Corporation or Censorship, whatever its advantages, would not have been a boon to England. In Italy, where the idea originated, the numerous Academies, so far from advancing the true interests of poetry, were largely instrumental in causing the artificiality and poverty of the 'Seicentisti.' Above all things it was considered necessary that the Italian poet should conform to rule: he always wrote with the thought of the Academy before his mind, and so his genius was hampered, his flights of fancy were confined to lines fixed by others. The French Academy, though different from institutions of the same name in Florence and Milan, was due to their example, and was founded in 1636. In England no less an authority than Milton recommended the establishment of a similar society to those which he had visited with so much pleasure in the company of his friend Diodati. His words are worth quoting:

"It were happy for the Commonwealth if our magistrates...would take into their care...the managing of our public sports and festival pastimes, that they might be such as...may civilize, adorn, and make discreet our minds, by the learned and affable meeting of frequent academies, and the procurement of wise and artful recitations;...whether this may be... at set and solemn paneguries, in theatres, porches or what other place or way may win most upon the people, to receive at once both recreation and instruction, let them in authority consult[1]."

The Earl of Roscommon, who had travelled in Italy during the Commonwealth, formed a plan for 'refining our language and fixing its standard,' and Dryden is

---

[1] *Reason of Church Government.*

said to have sympathized with his notions, which however, though taken up enthusiastically by some persons,
and revived, later on, by Dean Swift, never came to anything. It is not easy to say what would have been the
effect, if Milton's project—conceived in such a different
spirit from the whimsically-named clubs of dilettante
poets of Italy—could have been realized, but probably
we have not very much reason to regret its failure.
Perhaps the characteristic which most distinguishes the
great English poets of these centuries from the Italian
is the independence which, even when they are copying,
leads them to cast off the restraints of the original, and
to be impatient of the conventional fetters of so-called
decorum and good-taste, to which the Southerns yielded
so complacently. We cannot regret it. Let Shakspere
be 'barbarous' and 'wild.' Let Spenser be 'rustick'
and 'gothick.' Better so than to be unnatural and
affected. Better the rugged majesty of the honest
Teuton than the voluptuous effeminacy of the doubtful
Tuscan. Let Italy wear the laurel for graces of
symmetry, elegant correctness, and sweet melody;
England will be content with loving her poet-sons for
their kindly strength, their soaring fancy, and their
earnest purpose.

CONCLUSION.

It only remains to sum up. What is the net amount of our debt to Italy? Of course the influence exerted by and on a literature is not one that can be easily counted or weighed, but, as was said at the outset, it is possible to estimate pretty accurately what was the actual effect in this case, and this is because the Italian charm was so strong and lasting. First then in importance among the actual results we should be inclined to place the impetus given to our Drama, especially to Tragedy and the Romantic Comedy of Shakspere. The second place should perhaps be occupied by the fertile suggestions offered to Spenser and Milton. Not lower in the list must be put that expansion and enrichment of the resources of the vernacular which Italian refinement brought about; and immediately following this should be reckoned the prose Euphuism of Elizabeth's, and the poetical Euphuism of Charles I's reign. Then must be remembered the germs of prose fiction, the additions made to versification in the sonnet, the Spenserian stanza, and blank verse; the additions made to the vocabulary; the cultivation of quips, proverbs, anagrams and 'elegant sentences,' and the naturalization of the Pastoral. In fact it may be now asserted that

Italy gave us materials and colours, easel and paint-
brushes, set models and copies before us, and then left
us to paint our own pictures. She furnished our poets
with finer apparatus, and more attractive subjects than
they have ever had before or since. It was matter and
form that we derived from her; the spirit was our own.
Great as our obligations were, they do not detract from
the originality of the English Muse. The 'Italianate'
polish which sometimes obscured our authors' native
worth was only superficial; when that was rubbed off
the discovery was made how much better the plain
British oak was without such varnish. So the absurd
and objectionable fashions copied 'apishly' from Italy
passed away, and there was left behind the glorious
workmanship of all the noble thoughts and musical
strains that we associate with the names of Shakspere,
Spenser and Milton.